ANDERSON WILLAMS

The New Prepper's Water Survival Bible

Contents

Introduction   vii

1   Getting Started   1

2   Water Contamination and Purification   4

    Identifying Common Water Contaminants   4

    Effective Methods for Purifying Water   5

    Choosing the Right Water Filtration System   6

3   Essential Water Storage Strategies   8

    Selecting Appropriate Water Storage Containers   8

    Best Practices for Storing Water Long-Term   9

    Rotating and Maintaining Water Supplies   10

4   Rainwater Harvesting Techniques   12

    Setting up a Rainwater Collection System   12

    Filtering and Treating Rainwater for Consumption   13

    Integrating Rainwater Harvesting into
    Your Prepper Lifestyle   14

5   Underground Water Sources   16

    Locating and Tapping into Groundwater:
    Navigating Beneath the Surface   17

    Well Installation and Maintenance:
    Building and Sustaining the Lifeline   17

    Groundwater Filtration and Purification
    Methods: Unveiling Purity from Below   18

6   Emergency Water Sources in Nature   20

Identifying Safe Natural Water Sources: Nature's Nectar or Potential Peril?   20
Purifying Water from Streams, Lakes, and Rivers: Nature's Bounty, Refined for Consumption   21
Wilderness Survival Water Tips: Navigating the Aquatic Wilderness   23
Conclusion: Navigating the Waters of Wilderness Resilience   24

7 DIY Water Conservation and Recycling   26
Implementing Water-Saving Techniques: Nurturing a Thrifty Relationship with Water   27
Reusing and Recycling Water Resources: Crafting a Second Act for Water   28
Creating a Sustainable Water Usage Plan: Crafting a Blueprint for Responsibility   30

8 Portable Water Solutions for Bug-Out Scenarios   33
Compact Water Filtration and Purification Tools: Miniature Marvels for Hydration Assurance   34
Choosing the Right Portable Water Containers: The Crucial Vessels for Liquid Survival   35
Water Strategies for Evacuation: Navigating Fluidity in Urgency   36
Pre-planned Water Resupply Points: A Strategic Approach   37
Conservation Techniques: Maximizing Every Drop   37

Adaptability to Alternative Water
Sources: Embracing the Unexpected   38
Emergency Water Storage: A Backup
Plan for Assurance   38

9 Community Water Preparedness   40
Collaborative Approaches to Water Secu-
rity: The Strength of Unity   41
Establishing a Neighborhood Water Plan:
Blueprint for Community Resilience   42
Resources for Building Water-Resilient
Communities: A Well-Stocked Toolkit   45

10 Advanced Water Survival Skills   49
Mastering Alternative Water Procure-
ment: Beyond the Obvious Sources   50
Psychological Resilience in Water
Scarcity Challenges: The Mind as a
Survival Tool   51
Expert Tips for Extreme Water Emer-
gency Situations: Strategies for Unprece-
dented Challenges   52
Emergency Water Distillation Tech-
niques: Crafting Potable Water from
Unlikely Sources   53
Water Harvesting from Atmospheric
Sources: Navigating the Sky for Survival   53
Advanced Water Filtration: Safeguarding
Health in Unforgiving Environments   54
Evolving Your Water Prepping Skills for
the Future: Adapting to Changing Conditions   55
Sustainable Water Sourcing: A Paradigm
Shift in Prepping   55

Technological Integration for Water Resilience: Smart Solutions for Tomorrow   56
Community Collaboration for Water Security: Strengthening the Collective Front   57
11 Conclusion   60

Introduction

In a world where water is often taken for granted, the urgency of understanding and preparing for potential water crises has never been more critical. This introduction serves as the gateway into "The New Prepper's Water Survival Bible," a comprehensive guide designed to equip individuals and families with the knowledge and strategies needed to secure a sustainable water source in times of uncertainty.

Understanding the Importance of Water Preparedness

Water, the elixir of life, is central to our existence, yet its availability is not guaranteed. This section delves into the fundamental reasons behind the necessity of water preparedness. From the basic human need for hydration to the myriad uses of water in daily life, the reader is guided through an exploration of the profound impact that water scarcity can have on individuals and communities.

The narrative extends beyond personal survival, emphasizing the interconnectedness of water security with broader societal well-being. Understanding the importance of water preparedness becomes a journey of self-awareness and responsibility, where each individual's actions contribute to the collective resilience in the face of unpredictable circumstances

The Current Water Crisis: A Call to Action

As the specter of a global water crisis looms larger each day, this section provides an in-depth analysis of the current state of water scarcity worldwide. Through a blend of statistics, case studies, and real-world examples, readers are confronted with the stark realities of dwindling water resources and escalating demand.

The call to action resounds not only as a response to impending crises but as a proactive stance against complacency. Exploring the interconnected factors contributing to the water crisis, from climate change impacts to population growth, readers are motivated to become informed advocates for sustainable water management.

This section serves as a wake-up call, urging individuals to move beyond awareness and embrace a commitment to change. The call to action is not merely about personal preparedness; it's a rallying cry for collective responsibility and informed decision-making to secure a water-rich future.

In essence, this introduction lays the groundwork for an exploration into the depths of water preparedness. It intertwines the personal and the global, emphasizing that each person's understanding and actions contribute to the larger tapestry of water resilience. As readers embark on this journey through "The New Prepper's Water Survival Bible," they are empowered with knowledge and a sense of purpose to navigate the waters of uncertainty.

1

Getting Started

In emergency situations, the importance of water cannot be overstated. It serves as a fundamental resource for survival, playing a critical role in maintaining hydration, personal hygiene, and various essential household task. This section aims to underscore the significance of understanding and managing water resources in times of crisis.

Water scarcity can arise from various factors, including natural disasters, infrastructure failures, or unforeseen events that disrupt the regular supply. The repercussions of inadequate water supply can escalate rapidly, leading to health issues, sanitation problems, and an overall decline in the quality of life. Therefore, a proactive approach to water preparedness becomes paramount.

Understanding the intricacies of water in emergency situations involves recognizing potential threats to the water supply and being cognizant of the vulnerabilities in one's surroundings.

It requires a holistic comprehension of both short-term challenges, such as disruptions due to storms or power outages, and long-term scenarios, including prolonged droughts or infrastructure breakdowns.

Assessing your current water resources is the foundational step in effective water preparedness. It involves taking stock of the quantity and quality of water available to you in various contexts. This assessment encompasses an evaluation of your home's water sources, the reliability of local utilities, and the feasibility of alternative sources like wells or rainwater harvesting systems.

In urban settings, municipal water supplies are often the primary source. Understanding the resilience of this supply chain is crucial, considering factors such as the integrity of pipelines, treatment plants, and the overall infrastructure. For those in rural areas, reliance on well water or other local sources necessitates a thorough evaluation of well conditions, water quality testing, and potential risks associated with the specific water source.

A comprehensive assessment also involves understanding your household's water consumption patterns. This includes daily usage for drinking, cooking, bathing, and cleaning. By quantifying your water needs, you can better plan for storage requirements and develop strategies to conserve water during emergencies.

Moreover, getting started on water preparedness delves into the importance of recognizing early warning signs and staying informed about local water-related issues. This could involve monitoring weather forecasts, understanding seasonal variations, and participating in community initiatives focused on water resilience.

In summary, this section serves as the groundwork for navigating emergency situations. Understanding the critical role of water in such contexts, coupled with a thorough assessment of current water resources, lays the foundation for effective planning and resilience. As we delve deeper into specific aspects of water preparedness in subsequent sections, these foundational principles will guide us towards comprehensive and actionable strategies.

2

Water Contamination and Purification

Water contamination is a pressing concern that demands careful consideration, especially in the context of emergency preparedness. Understanding the types of contaminants that can compromise water safety is crucial for effective planning. This comprehensive exploration will delve into the various aspects of water contamination and purification, shedding light on common contaminants, purification methods, and the selection of appropriate water filtration systems.

Identifying Common Water Contaminants

Water contaminants pose significant threats to human health, and recognizing them is the first step in safeguarding water sources. Bacteria, viruses, parasites, chemicals, and heavy metals are among the primary culprits. Bacterial contaminants like E. coli and Salmonella can lead to severe gastrointestinal issues, while viruses such as Hepatitis A and norovirus can cause widespread illness. Parasites like Giardia and Cryptosporidium are waterborne pathogens that can resist conventional disinfection methods.

Chemical contaminants encompass a broad spectrum, including pesticides, industrial pollutants, and household chemicals. Heavy metals like lead, mercury, and arsenic can infiltrate water sources, posing long-term health risks. Understanding the sources and characteristics of these contaminants is vital for devising targeted purification strategies.

Effective Methods for Purifying Water

Purifying water is a multi-faceted process that involves the removal or inactivation of contaminants to meet safe consumption standards. Boiling water is a simple and effective method to eliminate many microbial contaminants, particularly bacteria and viruses. However, it may not be sufficient to address chemical pollutants or certain resilient pathogens.

Filtration is a widely employed technique that uses physical barriers to trap contaminants. Different types of filters, such as activated carbon filters and ceramic filters, target specific contaminants. Activated carbon is particularly effective in adsorbing organic chemicals and improving water taste. Meanwhile, ceramic filters with microscopic pores can remove bacteria and larger particles.

Chemical disinfection methods, including chlorination and iodine treatment, can effectively kill or inactivate a broad range of microorganisms. However, their efficacy may vary based on water quality, temperature, and contact time. Ultraviolet (UV) light treatment is another method gaining popularity for its ability to disrupt the DNA of microorganisms, rendering them unable to reproduce.

Choosing the Right Water Filtration System

Selecting an appropriate water filtration system is contingent on various factors, including the specific contaminants present, water source characteristics, and the intended use of the purified water. Point-of-use filters for individual households may differ from larger, community-level filtration systems.

Activated carbon filters are suitable for removing taste and odor issues, as well as certain organic chemicals. Reverse osmosis systems excel in eliminating a wide array of contaminants, including heavy metals and minerals. UV purifiers are effective against bacteria and viruses, making them valuable in scenarios where microbial contamination is a primary concern.

Consideration must also be given to the maintenance requirements, cost, and portability of filtration systems. In emergency situations, portable and easy-to-maintain options may be preferable. Moreover, understanding the limitations of each filtration method is crucial for making informed decisions and ensuring a reliable supply of safe drinking water.

In essence, an in-depth exploration of water contamination and purification reveals the complexity of safeguarding water quality in emergency situations. Identifying common contaminants, understanding purification methods, and selecting appropriate filtration systems form a comprehensive strategy for ensuring a reliable and safe water supply in times of need. This knowledge will empower individuals and communities to make informed choices and navigate water-related challenges effectively.

3

Essential Water Storage Strategies

Water storage is a critical component of emergency preparedness, ensuring a reliable and safe water supply during times
of scarcity or disruption. This comprehensive exploration
will delve into essential water storage strategies, covering the
selection of appropriate containers, best practices for long-term
storage, and the crucial aspects of rotating and maintaining
water supplies.

Selecting Appropriate Water Storage Containers

Choosing the right water storage containers is paramount to
maintaining water quality and safety. Containers must be
made from food-grade materials to prevent leaching of harmful
chemicals into the water. High-density polyethylene (HDPE)
containers are commonly recommended for their durability,
resistance to UV rays, and suitability for long-term water

storage.

The size of the containers also plays a crucial role. While larger containers can store more water, smaller containers offer advantages in terms of portability and ease of rotation. Moreover, containers with a tight-sealing lid or cap help prevent contamination and evaporation, ensuring the stored water remains potable.

Understanding the characteristics of different container materials is essential. For example, transparent containers may allow sunlight to penetrate, promoting algae growth and compromising water quality. Dark-colored or opaque containers are preferable for preventing light exposure.

Best Practices for Storing Water Long-Term

Storing water for the long term requires meticulous planning and adherence to best practices to guarantee its safety and potability. Prior to storage, it is crucial to thoroughly clean and sanitize containers to eliminate any contaminants. Chlorine bleach is often recommended for this purpose, ensuring the removal of bacteria and other pathogens.

Water should be sourced from a safe and reliable supply, and it is advisable to treat it before storage to minimize the risk of microbial growth. Adding chlorine or iodine in recommended concentrations can help disinfect the water. However, it's crucial to follow guidelines to avoid overtreating, which could lead to undesirable taste or other issues.

Temperature and storage location are also critical factors. Water should be stored in a cool, dark place to prevent the growth of algae and the degradation of container materials. Extreme temperatures can affect water quality, and freezing temperatures may damage containers. Adequate ventilation in storage areas is essential to prevent the buildup of potentially harmful gases.

Rotating and Maintaining Water Supplies

Regularly rotating stored water is a fundamental practice to ensure its freshness and potability. Water can become stale over time, developing off-flavors and odors. Rotating water supplies involves using and replacing stored water at regular intervals, preventing stagnation and microbial growth.

A systematic approach to rotating water supplies involves labeling containers with the storage date and implementing a first-in, first-out (FIFO) system. This ensures that older water is used before newer additions. The frequency of rotation depends on factors such as temperature, storage conditions, and the type of containers used.

Maintaining water supplies also involves periodic inspections and checks. Containers should be examined for signs of damage, leaks, or contamination. Any compromised containers should be replaced promptly. Additionally, water quality testing kits can be employed to assess the potability of stored water, providing peace of mind regarding its safety for consumption.

In summary, essential water storage strategies encompass selecting appropriate containers, adhering to best practices for long-term storage, and implementing systematic approaches to rotate and maintain water supplies. These practices are pivotal in ensuring a dependable and safe water source during emergency situations. As we navigate the nuances of water storage, these fundamental principles will guide us toward building resilience and preparedness in the face of water scarcity or disruptions.

4

Rainwater Harvesting Techniques

Rainwater harvesting is a sustainable and effective method for securing a supplementary water source, especially in emergency preparedness scenarios. This comprehensive exploration will delve into rainwater harvesting techniques, covering the setup of a rainwater collection system, the importance of filtering and treating rainwater for consumption, and practical strategies for integrating rainwater harvesting into a prepper lifestyle.

Setting up a Rainwater Collection System

The foundation of rainwater harvesting lies in the setup of a well-designed collection system. The first step involves identifying suitable surfaces for rainwater collection, such as rooftops. The size and slope of the collection surface directly impact the quantity of rainwater that can be harvested. Ideally, non-toxic roofing materials should be chosen to minimize the risk of contaminants in the collected water.

Gutters and downspouts play a crucial role in directing rainwater from the collection surface to storage containers. Installing a mesh or leaf guard on gutters prevents debris from entering the system, ensuring cleaner water. Downspouts should be strategically placed to maximize water flow and minimize splashing.

Storage containers are a key component of the rainwater collection system. These can range from simple barrels to more sophisticated tanks. The choice of container material, such as food-grade polyethylene, and proper installation are essential for maintaining water quality. Elevating containers off the ground can facilitate gravity-driven water flow, simplifying distribution.

Filtering and Treating Rainwater for Consumption

While rainwater is generally considered pure, it can still contain contaminants picked up from the atmosphere or collection surfaces. Filtering and treating rainwater are essential steps to ensure it meets safe drinking standards.

A first-flush diverter is a valuable addition to a rainwater harvesting system, diverting the initial runoff, which may contain pollutants accumulated on the collection surface. Additionally, installing a leaf filter or mesh at the entry point of the collection system prevents debris from entering storage containers.

Treating rainwater involves addressing potential microbial contaminants. Ultraviolet (UV) disinfection systems are effective in neutralizing bacteria and viruses, providing an additional layer of protection. Boiling rainwater is also a simple and reliable method for disinfection, particularly in emergency situations.

Chemical treatments, such as chlorine or iodine, can be used for disinfection, but dosage must be carefully controlled to avoid undesirable taste or health risks. Regular testing of treated rainwater for microbial content ensures the ongoing effectiveness of the chosen treatment method.

Integrating Rainwater Harvesting into Your Prepper Lifestyle

Adopting rainwater harvesting into a prepper lifestyle requires a holistic approach that considers both daily water needs and long-term sustainability. Rainwater can be integrated into various aspects of life, from drinking and cooking to gardening and hygiene.

In the home, rainwater can supplement municipal or well water for non-potable uses like laundry, flushing toilets, and watering plants. Rain barrels strategically placed near gardens or greenhouses provide a sustainable water source for plants, reducing reliance on conventional water supplies.

Educating yourself and your community about rainwater harvesting fosters a culture of self-sufficiency. Workshops, online resources, and community initiatives can promote the benefits of rainwater harvesting, encouraging widespread adoption and resilience.

For preppers, rainwater harvesting aligns with the ethos of self-reliance and preparedness. Developing contingency plans for optimizing rainwater collection during different seasons, maintaining the collection system, and regularly reviewing water storage practices ensures readiness for unpredictable scenarios.

In essence, rainwater harvesting techniques encompass setting up an efficient collection system, filtering and treating rainwater for consumption, and integrating this sustainable practice into a prepper lifestyle. By understanding the nuances of rainwater harvesting and implementing best practices, individuals and communities can enhance their water resilience and contribute to a more sustainable and self-sufficient future.

5

Underground Water Sources

Underground water sources, commonly referred to as ground-water, are invaluable reservoirs that contribute significantly to global water availability. Understanding the dynamics of locating, tapping into, and managing groundwater is essential for ensuring a sustainable and reliable water supply. This comprehensive exploration will delve into the intricacies of underground water sources, providing insights into the methods of locating and tapping into groundwater, the installation and maintenance of wells, and the filtration and purification methods necessary for ensuring the safety of groundwater.

Locating and Tapping into Groundwater: Navigating Beneath the Surface

Locating underground water sources involves a combination of geological knowledge, hydrological studies, and technology. Geological features such as rock formations, soil types, and the presence of certain vegetation can indicate the potential for groundwater. Geophysical methods, including seismic surveys and ground-penetrating radar, are instrumental in mapping subsurface structures and identifying aquifers.

Once a potential site is identified, tapping into groundwater requires the installation of wells. The process involves drilling or digging to reach the water-bearing strata beneath the ground. The choice of well type—such as dug wells, driven wells, or drilled wells—depends on factors like geological conditions, depth to the water table, and the intended use of the water.

Well Installation and Maintenance: Building and Sustaining the Lifeline

The installation of a well is a critical step in accessing underground water. Dug wells, typically excavated by hand or machinery, are common in shallow aquifers. Driven wells involve hammering a casing into the ground, while drilled wells use rotary or percussion drilling to reach deeper aquifers. Each method has its advantages and considerations, necessitating careful evaluation based on geological characteristics and water needs.

Maintenance of wells is crucial for sustaining their efficiency and ensuring the quality of extracted groundwater. Regular inspections for signs of contamination, structural integrity, and the functionality of well components are essential. Sealing and grouting the well properly prevent surface water from infiltrating and compromising the purity of groundwater. Protective measures, such as well caps and casings, safeguard against pollutants and the entry of debris.

Groundwater Filtration and Purification Methods: Unveiling Purity from Below

While groundwater is generally considered cleaner than surface water, it can still harbor contaminants that pose health risks. Filtration and purification methods are employed to enhance the safety and quality of extracted groundwater.

Filtration involves the removal of suspended particles and impurities. Sand filters, sediment filters, and cartridge filters are commonly used in well systems to trap debris and prevent it from entering the water supply. Choosing the appropriate filter depends on factors like the size of particles and the specific characteristics of the aquifer.

Purification methods focus on eliminating microbial contaminants and chemical impurities. Chlorination, a widely adopted method, involves adding chlorine to the well to disinfect the water and kill harmful bacteria. UV disinfection is another effective method, utilizing ultraviolet light to neutralize pathogens without introducing chemicals or altering water taste.

Activated carbon filters are employed to remove organic compounds and improve water taste. Reverse osmosis systems, which use a semi-permeable membrane to separate impurities, are effective in eliminating a broad spectrum of contaminants, including minerals and heavy metals.

In summary, the exploration of underground water sources unveils a world beneath the surface, offering a lifeline for sustainable water security. Locating and tapping into groundwater demand a nuanced understanding of geological and hydrological factors, while well installation and maintenance are pivotal for sustaining this vital resource. The filtration and purification methods applied to groundwater ensure that the water extracted is not only abundant but also safe for consumption. As we navigate the depths to access and manage underground water, the principles outlined in this comprehensive exploration will guide individuals and communities towards building resilience and security in their water supply.

6

Emergency Water Sources in Nature

When faced with emergency situations in the great outdoors, the ability to identify and utilize natural water sources is paramount for survival. This comprehensive exploration will delve into the nuances of emergency water sources in nature, emphasizing the identification of safe water sources, effective methods for purifying water from streams, lakes, and rivers, and practical wilderness survival water tips.

Identifying Safe Natural Water Sources: Nature's Nectar or Potential Peril?

In the wild, the availability of water is diverse, ranging from seemingly pristine streams to stagnant ponds. However, not all water sources are safe for consumption, and identifying the difference between potable and potentially hazardous water is a crucial skill for anyone venturing into the wilderness.

Safe natural water sources often exhibit characteristics that set them apart. Flowing water, like that in streams or rivers, is generally less likely to be contaminated than stagnant water. Clear water is preferable, as turbidity or discoloration may indicate the presence of impurities. Examining the surrounding environment for signs of pollution or industrial activity is essential in making informed decisions about water safety.

Wildlife can be an indicator of water quality; animals are often selective about the water they drink. However, caution is needed, as wildlife may have different tolerance levels for contaminants. Learning to read the landscape and understanding the interconnectedness of ecosystems aids in identifying water sources that are more likely to be safe for consumption.

Purifying Water from Streams, Lakes, and Rivers: Nature's Bounty, Refined for Consumption

While identifying safe water sources is the first step, purifying water from streams, lakes, and rivers is equally critical to ensure its safety for consumption. Various methods can be employed to remove or neutralize contaminants present in natural water sources.

Boiling water is one of the oldest and most reliable methods of purification. By bringing water to a rolling boil for a specified period, usually a few minutes, harmful bacteria, viruses, and parasites are effectively eliminated. This method is especially effective in emergency situations when minimal equipment is available.

Filtration is another widely used method, utilizing physical barriers to trap impurities. Portable water filters equipped with ceramic or activated carbon elements can be effective in removing sediment, bacteria, and other contaminants. It's essential to choose filters with a suitable pore size to address the specific threats present in the water source.

Chemical purification methods, such as water purification tablets or drops containing chlorine or iodine, offer convenient solutions for on-the-go water treatment. These chemicals are effective in neutralizing many microorganisms, but the taste and odor of the treated water may be affected.

Ultraviolet (UV) light devices are becoming increasingly popular for wilderness water purification. These handheld devices use UV rays to disrupt the DNA of microorganisms, rendering them unable to reproduce. While effective against bacteria and viruses, UV purifiers do not remove physical impurities, necessitating additional filtration in some cases.

Wilderness Survival Water Tips: Navigating the Aquatic Wilderness

Surviving in the wilderness requires a holistic approach to water procurement and consumption. Wilderness survival water tips encompass a range of practices aimed at ensuring a sustainable and safe water supply, even in challenging conditions.

Carrying an emergency water supply is a fundamental tip for wilderness survival. Whether through portable water bottles, hydration packs, or collapsible containers, having a reserve of treated and purified water provides a vital buffer against unexpected situations. Additionally, understanding the rate of water consumption based on exertion levels, climate, and individual needs is crucial for rationing and planning.

Mapping out water sources in advance is a proactive strategy. Before venturing into the wilderness, studying topographic maps, guidebooks, and local knowledge can help identify reliable water sources along the route. This pre-planning reduces the reliance on uncertain water-finding expeditions during critical moments.

Implementing water conservation practices is essential in the wild, where resources may be limited. Cooking with minimal water, reusing water for multiple purposes, and avoiding unnecessary water wastage contribute to sustainable water management. Hygiene practices, though crucial, should also be mindful of water conservation principles.

Incorporating natural indicators into water-finding strategies enhances survival skills. Observing vegetation patterns, animal behavior, and terrain characteristics can provide insights into the proximity of water sources. Learning about specific plant species that may indicate water availability adds another layer to one's survival toolkit.

Finally, continually refining one's knowledge and skills related to wilderness water survival is an ongoing process. Staying informed about new water purification technologies, practicing water procurement techniques, and participating in survival training programs contribute to a robust skill set that can make a significant difference in emergency situations.

Conclusion: Navigating the Waters of Wilderness Resilience

In conclusion, the exploration of emergency water sources in nature unveils a dynamic and essential aspect of wilderness survival. Identifying safe natural water sources requires a blend of observation, environmental awareness, and ecological understanding. Purifying water from streams, lakes, and rivers involves deploying a repertoire of methods suited to the unique challenges posed by each water source.

Wilderness survival water tips encapsulate a holistic approach to water resilience, emphasizing preparation, conservation, and ongoing education. As individuals venture into the great outdoors, equipped with the knowledge gained from this comprehensive exploration, they not only ensure their own survival but contribute to a deeper understanding and appreciation of nature's aquatic bounty

7

DIY Water Conservation and Recycling

As global awareness of water scarcity grows, the need for sustainable water practices becomes increasingly evident. DIY water conservation and recycling offer pragmatic solutions for individuals and households to contribute to the preservation of this precious resource. This comprehensive exploration will delve into the intricacies of implementing water-saving techniques, reusing and recycling water resources, and creating a sustainable water usage plan within the realm of accessible do-it-yourself initiatives.

Implementing Water-Saving Techniques: Nurturing a Thrifty Relationship with Water

The foundation of DIY water conservation lies in the implementation of water-saving techniques within daily activities. Simple yet effective practices can significantly reduce water consumption, easing the burden on local water supplies and contributing to a more sustainable future.

Upgrading to water-efficient fixtures is a tangible starting point. Installing low-flow faucets and showerheads can substantially decrease water usage without compromising functionality. Similarly, opting for dual-flush toilets or retrofitting existing toilets with water-saving devices provides an immediate impact on water conservation.

Mindful landscaping practices play a pivotal role in DIY water conservation. Choosing native and drought-resistant plants reduces the need for extensive watering. Utilizing mulch around plants helps retain soil moisture, minimizing evaporation and promoting healthier growth. Implementing rain barrels to collect and store rainwater for garden irrigation further reduces reliance on municipal water sources.

Regular maintenance of household appliances is often overlooked but crucial for water efficiency. Fixing leaks promptly, ensuring appliances are operating optimally, and replacing worn-out parts contribute to a more water-conscious home. DIY enthusiasts can explore simple plumbing repairs and maintenance tasks to minimize water wastage.

Embracing behavioral changes within the household is fundamental to DIY water conservation. Turning off the tap while brushing teeth, using dishwashers and washing machines only when fully loaded, and fixing leaky faucets are small yet impactful adjustments. Building awareness within the household about the value of water and the impact of individual habits fosters a collective commitment to water conservation.

Reusing and Recycling Water Resources: Crafting a Second Act for Water

Beyond reducing consumption, DIY water conservation extends to reusing and recycling water resources, maximizing the utility of water within the confines of a home. Creative and practical initiatives can transform water from a single-use commodity into a valuable resource with multiple applications.

Greywater recycling is a DIY strategy gaining popularity. Greywater, wastewater generated from domestic activities like laundry, bathing, and dishwashing, can be treated and repurposed for non-potable uses. DIY greywater systems, ranging from simple diversion methods to more sophisticated filtration setups, allow households to harness this resource for garden irrigation or flushing toilets.

Rainwater harvesting complements greywater recycling, providing an additional avenue for reusing water resources. DIY rainwater harvesting systems can range from basic rain barrels connected to downspouts to more elaborate setups with filtration systems. Capturing and utilizing rainwater for non-potable needs further reduces the demand on conventional water sources.

DIY enthusiasts can explore the potential of constructed wetlands for water treatment on a smaller scale. These miniature ecosystems mimic natural wetlands, providing a natural and aesthetically pleasing method to filter and treat greywater for reuse. Proper design and plant selection ensure the effectiveness of the system in improving water quality.

Innovative DIY projects can turn discarded household items into water-saving devices. For example, repurposing a plastic bottle into a drip irrigation system or using reclaimed materials to build a rain garden showcases the creativity inherent in reusing and recycling water resources at the individual level.

Creating a Sustainable Water Usage Plan: Crafting a Blueprint for Responsibility

The pinnacle of DIY water conservation lies in creating a sustainable water usage plan tailored to the unique needs and circumstances of a household. This proactive approach involves thoughtful consideration of water sources, usage patterns, and long-term objectives.

Assessing the water footprint of daily activities is a foundational step in creating a sustainable water usage plan. Understanding how much water is used for different tasks allows for targeted conservation efforts. DIY water audits, involving the monitoring of water consumption and identifying inefficiencies, empower individuals to make informed decisions about resource management.

Establishing a water budget is a practical component of a DIY water usage plan. Setting realistic goals for water consumption based on household size, local climate, and available water sources provides a framework for accountability. Periodic evaluations help track progress and make necessary adjustments to achieve sustainability targets.

Incorporating smart technology into water management enhances DIY water conservation efforts. Smart irrigation systems, moisture sensors, and water-efficient appliances can be integrated into a sustainable water usage plan. DIY installation and maintenance of these technologies contribute to a more intelligent and resource-efficient home.

Educating household members about the importance of water conservation and the specifics of the sustainable water usage plan fosters a culture of responsibility. DIY water education can include workshops, informational materials, and hands-on activities to engage everyone in the household in the journey towards sustainability.

Collaborating with the community amplifies the impact of individual DIY water conservation efforts. Participating in local water conservation initiatives, sharing DIY projects with neighbors, and contributing to community water awareness programs create a network of support and inspiration. DIY enthusiasts can organize workshops or events to share knowledge and skills, cultivating a shared commitment to water sustainability.

In essence, DIY water conservation and recycling epitomize the transformative power of individual actions in addressing global challenges. Implementing water-saving techniques, reusing and recycling water resources, and creating a sustainable water usage plan are not just pragmatic measures but powerful contributions to a sustainable and responsible future.

The journey towards DIY water wisdom involves a blend of innovation, education, and daily mindfulness. As individuals embark on the path of DIY water conservation, they become stewards of this vital resource, weaving a tapestry of responsibility that extends from their homes to the broader community. Through the lens of DIY initiatives, water conservation becomes a personal endeavor, a craft honed with care and a legacy of sustainability crafted for generations to come

8

Portable Water Solutions for Bug-Out Scenarios

In the realm of emergency preparedness, particularly in bug-out scenarios where swift evacuation is essential, having reliable portable water solutions is paramount. This comprehensive exploration will delve into the intricacies of compact water filtration and purification tools, the selection of appropriate portable water containers, and strategic water management for effective evacuation.

Compact Water Filtration and Purification Tools: Miniature Marvels for Hydration Assurance

In bug-out scenarios, where space and weight are critical considerations, compact water filtration and purification tools emerge as indispensable assets. These miniature marvels are designed to address the immediate need for safe and potable water in transient and unpredictable environments.

Portable water filters, equipped with advanced filtration technologies, are instrumental in removing contaminants from various water sources. The design often incorporates a hand-pump or squeeze mechanism, allowing users to manually filter water as needed. Filters with micron-sized pores effectively capture bacteria, protozoa, and sediment, providing a reliable first line of defense against waterborne threats.

Water purification tablets or drops offer a chemical-based approach to rendering water safe for consumption. These compact solutions typically contain chlorine or iodine, which, when added to water, neutralize harmful microorganisms. While not as instantaneous as filtration, purification tablets are lightweight, easy to carry, and suitable for bug-out scenarios where minimal equipment is preferable.

Ultraviolet (UV) light purifiers have gained popularity for their efficiency in microbial disinfection. These handheld devices use UV rays to disrupt the DNA of bacteria, viruses, and other pathogens, rendering them incapable of reproduction. Compact and battery-operated, UV purifiers offer a quick and reliable method for water disinfection in bug-out situations.

Survival straws are another innovation in compact water filtration. These portable devices allow users to drink directly
from water sources by filtering out impurities as the water is
drawn through the straw. With built-in filters, survival straws
are designed to be lightweight and easy to carry, making them
suitable for bug-out scenarios where mobility is a priority.

Choosing the Right Portable Water Containers: The Crucial Vessels for Liquid Survival

Selecting the appropriate portable water containers is a pivotal
aspect of bug-out preparedness. The chosen vessels must strike
a balance between durability, weight, and capacity, ensuring an
efficient and reliable means of carrying water during evacuation.

Collapsible water containers are favored for their space-saving
design. These containers can be flattened or rolled up when
empty, allowing users to maximize storage efficiency during
transport. Commonly made from flexible materials like BPA-
free plastics, collapsible water containers are lightweight and
come in various sizes to suit individual or group needs.

Stainless steel water bottles are renowned for their durability
and resistance to impact. In bug-out scenarios, where rugged
conditions may be encountered, stainless steel bottles provide a

robust option for carrying water. Additionally, their insulation properties can keep water cool, offering a refreshing sip even in challenging environments.

Hydration bladders, often integrated into backpacks or worn as standalone systems, are ideal for bug-out scenarios where continuous movement is essential. These bladder systems feature a flexible reservoir with a drinking tube, allowing users to stay hydrated on the go. The hands-free design is especially advantageous during evacuation, ensuring that water is readily accessible without the need to stop.

Canteens with nesting cups or multi-functional designs are versatile options for bug-out scenarios. These containers often feature additional compartments or accessories, such as purification tablets or a built-in filtration system. The nesting cups can serve dual purposes for cooking or heating water, adding to the overall utility of the canteen.

Water Strategies for Evacuation: Navigating Fluidity in Urgency

In bug-out scenarios, where swift evacuation is the primary objective, effective water management strategies are crucial for ensuring hydration while on the move. These strategies encompass planning, conservation, and adaptability to dynamic conditions.

Pre-planned Water Resupply Points: A Strategic Approach

In bug-out scenarios, having pre-planned water resupply points along the evacuation route is a strategic approach. Identifying reliable water sources in advance, such as streams, rivers, or known natural springs, allows evacuees to optimize their travel routes based on water availability. This proactive measure minimizes uncertainty and ensures a strategic and informed approach to water resupply during evacuation.

Conservation Techniques: Maximizing Every Drop

Conservation of water becomes paramount in bug-out scenarios, where the availability of water is uncertain, and resources must be maximized. Implementing water-saving practices, such as rationing water consumption, using efficient hydration techniques, and minimizing non-essential water use, ensures that the available water lasts throughout the evacuation journey. Conservation becomes a mindset, influencing every decision related to water consumption and contributing to the overall success of the bug-out strategy.

Adaptability to Alternative Water Sources: Embracing the Unexpected

Bug-out scenarios can be unpredictable, and the availability of potable water may vary. Evacuees must be prepared to adapt to alternative water sources, such as rainwater, dew, or even unconventional sources with proper purification. Portable filtration and purification tools become indispensable in this context, offering the flexibility to obtain safe drinking water from a range of sources encountered during evacuation.

Emergency Water Storage: A Backup Plan for Assurance

As part of bug-out preparedness, having a compact emergency water storage system adds an additional layer of assurance. Portable water containers with built-in filtration or purification capabilities can be filled before evacuation, providing a backup supply of safe drinking water. This ensures that evacuees have immediate access to a reliable water source, especially in situations where resupply may be delayed or uncertain.

In summary, navigating hydration challenges in bug-out scenarios requires a holistic approach encompassing compact water filtration tools, appropriate portable containers, and strategic water management. The selection of tools and containers should align with the priorities of mobility, efficiency, and adaptability to dynamic conditions.

As individuals and communities embrace the urgency of bug-out preparedness, incorporating portable water solutions becomes a foundational element in ensuring resilience and survival. Through informed choices, strategic planning, and the integration of portable water tools into bug-out strategies, individuals can navigate hydration challenges with confidence, knowing that a reliable source of safe drinking water is always within reach during evacuation.

9

Community Water Preparedness

In the intricate tapestry of community preparedness, ensuring a resilient and secure water supply stands as a cornerstone. This comprehensive exploration will delve into collaborative approaches to water security, the establishment of neighborhood water plans, and the rich array of resources available for building water-resilient communities. As communities face the challenges of a changing climate, population growth, and potential disruptions, forging a collective commitment to water preparedness becomes an imperative thread in the fabric of overall resilience.

Collaborative Approaches to Water Security: The Strength of Unity

Water security at the community level hinges on collaborative approaches that harness the strength of unity. Collective efforts enable communities to pool resources, share knowledge, and build comprehensive strategies for sustained water availability. Initiatives that foster collaboration among community members, local authorities, and relevant stakeholders become linchpins in achieving water security.

Establishing water committees within communities is a fundamental step toward collaboration. These committees bring together individuals with diverse skills, knowledge, and perspectives to collectively address water-related challenges. From engineers and hydrologists to community organizers and residents, a multidisciplinary approach ensures that the water committee is well-equipped to tackle the multifaceted aspects of water security.

Collaboration extends beyond community borders through regional partnerships. Establishing networks with neighboring communities, local government agencies, and non-profit organizations creates a support system for sharing best practices, resources, and emergency response plans. This interconnectedness fosters a sense of shared responsibility and enhances the overall resilience of the region.

Engaging in collaborative research and data sharing empowers communities with a deeper understanding of local water resources. By pooling information on groundwater levels, river flow patterns, and climate projections, communities can make informed decisions about sustainable water management. This collaborative knowledge-sharing approach becomes particularly critical in adapting to changing environmental conditions and planning for long-term water security.

Establishing a Neighborhood Water Plan: Blueprint for Community Resilience

A neighborhood water plan serves as a blueprint for community resilience, outlining strategies and actions to ensure a secure and sustainable water supply. Developing and implementing such a plan requires active participation from community members, local authorities, and experts. The following elements contribute to the establishment of an effective neighborhood water plan.

Assessment of Water Resources:

Understanding local water resources is the foundation of a neighborhood water plan. Conducting a comprehensive assessment of groundwater availability, surface water sources, and potential risks of contamination provides a clear picture of the community's water landscape. This assessment guides subsequent planning efforts and informs strategies for sustainable water use.

Identification of Vulnerabilities:

Examining vulnerabilities in the water supply chain is a crucial step. This includes assessing the susceptibility of water sources to climate-related changes, potential contamination sources, and vulnerabilities in the water distribution infrastructure. Identifying these vulnerabilities enables communities to proactively address weak points and fortify their water resilience.

Community Engagement and Education:

Engaging the community in the water planning process is paramount. Educational initiatives on water conservation, sustainable usage practices, and emergency preparedness foster a sense of shared responsibility. Workshops, community meetings, and educational campaigns create a well-informed populace that actively contributes to and supports the implementation of the neighborhood water plan.

Infrastructure Development and Maintenance:

Investing in resilient water infrastructure is a key component of the neighborhood water plan. This involves ensuring the integrity of water supply systems, pipelines, and treatment facilities. Implementing water-saving technologies and adopting green infrastructure practices contribute to sustainable water management. Regular maintenance schedules and swift responses to infrastructure issues enhance the overall reliability of the water supply.

Emergency Response and Contingency Planning: Anticipating and planning for emergencies is integral to a robust neighborhood water plan. Establishing contingency measures, such as emergency water storage, alternative water sources, and community-wide communication strategies, ensures that the community can respond effectively to disruptions in the water supply. Regular drills and simulations prepare residents for various scenarios, fostering a resilient mindset.

Integration of Technology:

Leveraging technology enhances the effectiveness of a neighborhood water plan. Implementing sensor networks for monitoring water quality, utilizing data analytics for demand forecasting, and employing smart metering systems contribute to efficient water management. Technology facilitates real-time data collection, enabling communities to respond promptly to changing conditions and optimize their water resources.

Resources for Building Water-Resilient Communities: A Well-Stocked Toolkit

Building water-resilient communities involves tapping into a well-stocked toolkit of resources that encompass knowledge, technology, and community engagement. A comprehensive approach to resource utilization ensures that communities are equipped to face current challenges and anticipate future uncertainties.

Educational Resources:

Educational materials on water conservation, sustainable usage, and emergency preparedness serve as foundational resources. Community libraries, online platforms, and local workshops can provide residents with the information they need to understand the importance of water resilience and adopt practices that contribute to it.

Training Programs:

Training programs, conducted by experts in water management, emergency response, and community organizing, offer communities the opportunity to build specific skills. Workshops on rainwater harvesting, water quality testing, and infrastructure maintenance empower residents to actively contribute to water resilience. These programs foster a culture of continuous learning and skill development within the community.

Government Grants and Funding:

Government grants and funding opportunities are critical resources for implementing water resilience projects. Communities can explore grants provided by federal, state, or local agencies to support infrastructure upgrades, research initiatives, and educational campaigns. Leveraging these financial resources enables communities to implement comprehensive water resilience strategies.

Collaborative Research Initiatives:

Participating in collaborative research initiatives facilitates access to cutting-edge knowledge and expertise. Universities, research institutions, and non-profit organizations often initiate projects focused on water resilience. By engaging with such initiatives, communities gain insights into innovative technologies, data-driven strategies, and emerging best practices in the field.

Technological Solutions:

Technological resources, ranging from water monitoring systems to data analytics tools, contribute to effective water management. Communities can explore partnerships with technology providers, utilize open-source platforms, or invest in custom solutions tailored to their specific needs. Incorporating technology into water resilience efforts enhances the efficiency of monitoring, forecasting, and response mechanisms.

Community-Based Organizations:

Community-based organizations play a crucial role in building water-resilient communities. Non-profit groups focused on environmental conservation, water access, and community development can provide support, expertise, and networking opportunities. Collaborating with these organizations strengthens community initiatives and expands the reach of water resilience efforts.

In essence, community water preparedness is a multifaceted endeavor that requires collaboration, planning, and the strategic utilization of resources. By embracing collaborative approaches to water security, communities fortify themselves against the challenges posed by climate variability, population growth, and potential disruptions in water supply.

Establishing a neighborhood water plan serves as the guiding thread in this tapestry of water resilience, offering a structured and proactive approach to sustainable water management. Through community engagement, infrastructure development, and contingency planning, neighborhoods weave a robust framework that can withstand uncertainties and adapt to changing conditions.

The toolkit for building water-resilient communities is diverse and rich, encompassing educational resources, training programs, government support, collaborative research initiatives, technological solutions, and the strength of community-based organizations. By tapping into this well-stocked toolkit, communities empower themselves to navigate the complex landscape of water security and emerge stronger and more resilient drop by drop.

10

Advanced Water Survival Skills

In the realm of water survival, mastering advanced skills goes beyond the basics, offering a heightened level of preparedness for diverse and challenging situations. This comprehensive exploration will delve into the intricacies of advanced water survival skills, addressing not only the physical aspects of water sourcing but also the mental fortitude required to navigate extreme conditions. From mastering alternative water procurement methods to understanding the psychological aspects of survival, advanced water survival skills nurture expertise in hydration resilience, ensuring individuals can thrive in even the most demanding scenarios.

Mastering Alternative Water Procurement: Beyond the Obvious Sources

Advanced water survival skills require a nuanced understanding of alternative water procurement methods, especially in environments where traditional sources may be scarce or compromised. Beyond obvious sources like rivers, lakes, and wells, individuals must explore unconventional avenues for securing this life-sustaining resource.

One advanced technique involves harvesting water from vegetation. Certain plants, such as succulents, can be sources of potable water. Extracting moisture from plant tissues or utilizing transpiration bags to collect evaporated water from leaves requires knowledge and precision. Mastering these skills broadens the spectrum of potential water sources in arid or unconventional landscapes.

Solar stills represent another advanced method for extracting water from non-liquid sources. By utilizing the sun's energy to induce condensation, individuals can convert moisture from damp soil, vegetation, or even urine into drinkable water. While the process requires patience and the right environmental conditions, mastering solar still techniques can be a game-changer in survival situations.

Desalination, traditionally considered a complex and energy-intensive process, has advanced to become more accessible. Portable desalination devices powered by solar energy or hand-crank mechanisms offer a solution for obtaining freshwater from seawater. Understanding the intricacies of these devices and incorporating them into a survival toolkit expands the scope of water procurement options, especially for those navigating coastal or marine environments.

Psychological Resilience in Water Scarcity Challenges: The Mind as a Survival Tool

Surviving in water-scarce environments demands not only physical resilience but also psychological fortitude. Advanced water survival skills encompass understanding and leveraging the mental aspects of survival, recognizing the profound impact of mindset on decision-making and overall well-being.

Psychological resilience begins with the ability to manage stress and anxiety associated with water scarcity. Techniques such as mindfulness, meditation, and controlled breathing become invaluable tools in maintaining focus and emotional balance. Cultivating these skills equips individuals to navigate challenging situations with a clear and centered mind.

The ability to adapt to uncertainty and embrace a positive mindset is paramount. In water-scarce environments, where the outcome is uncertain and resources are limited, maintaining optimism and adaptability becomes a survival strategy. Advanced water survival skills involve training the mind to see opportunities in adversity and creatively problem-solve in the face of scarcity.

Understanding the psychological impact of dehydration is crucial. Dehydration can impair cognitive function, leading to poor decision-making and diminished problem-solving abilities. Individuals with advanced water survival skills recognize the early signs of dehydration and prioritize hydration not only for physical well-being but also for maintaining mental acuity in critical situations.

Expert Tips for Extreme Water Emergency Situations: Strategies for Unprecedented Challenges

In extreme water emergency situations, where conventional resources may be entirely depleted, expert tips become lifelines for survival. These advanced strategies go beyond basic prepping and demand a comprehensive understanding of water dynamics, resourcefulness, and adaptability to unforeseen challenges.

Emergency Water Distillation Techniques: Crafting Potable Water from Unlikely Sources

In scenarios where no immediate water sources are available, emergency water distillation becomes a crucial skill. This advanced technique involves creating makeshift distillation setups to extract freshwater from contaminated or saline sources. Building improvised solar stills using readily available materials, such as plastic sheets or bags, enables individuals to distill water through the natural process of evaporation and condensation.

The art of emergency water distillation extends to creating DIY solar water stills. By harnessing the sun's energy, individuals can distill water in small quantities, providing a reliable source of safe drinking water. Understanding the principles of condensation, surface tension, and heat transfer is essential for mastering this technique.

Water Harvesting from Atmospheric Sources: Navigating the Sky for Survival

In extreme water emergency situations, where traditional sources are exhausted, individuals must turn to unconventional methods such as harvesting water from atmospheric sources. Techniques like dew harvesting involve collecting moisture from the air during the cooler hours of the night. Utilizing dew condensation traps or improvised collection surfaces, individuals can amass small but vital quantities of water.

Cloud seeding, although typically an industrial process, can be adapted in extreme survival situations. By creating simple devices to encourage condensation, individuals may capture water droplets from passing clouds. This expert-level strategy demands a deep understanding of meteorological conditions and cloud dynamics.

Advanced Water Filtration: Safeguarding Health in Unforgiving Environments

Extreme emergency situations may expose individuals to water sources contaminated with pollutants or pathogens. Advanced water filtration skills are paramount for safeguarding health in such unforgiving environments. Understanding the capabilities and limitations of various filtration methods ensures the production of safe and potable water.

Activated carbon filtration, in addition to traditional methods, becomes an advanced technique for removing chemical contaminants. Activated carbon filters, with their high adsorption capacity, effectively capture organic and inorganic impurities, improving water quality. Individuals with advanced water filtration skills are adept at integrating activated carbon into their portable filtration systems.

Improvised ceramic water filters are another expert-level strategy for removing bacteria and sediment from water. Crafting these filters using locally available materials, such as clay and sawdust, demonstrates resourcefulness in extreme conditions. Understanding the principles of filtration and mastering the construction of improvised ceramic filters enhance survival capabilities.

Evolving Your Water Prepping Skills for the Future: Adapting to Changing Conditions

As the world grapples with the impacts of climate change and evolving environmental conditions, evolving water prepping skills for the future is a strategic imperative. Advanced prepping involves not only mastering traditional survival techniques but also adapting to the dynamic nature of global challenges. From embracing sustainable practices to harnessing technology, individuals must anticipate future needs and build resilient water prepping strategies.

Sustainable Water Sourcing: A Paradigm Shift in Prepping

In the face of changing climate patterns and increased environmental stress, a paradigm shift toward sustainable water sourcing becomes essential for future prepping. This involves exploring regenerative practices that contribute to water conservation and ecosystem health. Rainwater harvesting, permaculture design principles, and responsible water usage are integral components of sustainable water prepping.

Rainwater harvesting, as an advanced prepping technique, involves capturing and storing rainwater for future use. Implementing efficient rainwater collection systems, such as rooftop harvesting or integrated catchment basins, ensures a supplementary water source during periods of scarcity. Advanced rainwater harvesting practices include optimizing storage capacity and incorporating filtration methods to enhance water quality.

Permaculture design principles offer a holistic approach to water-conscious living. By integrating water management strategies into the design of landscapes and habitats, individuals can create self-sustaining ecosystems that optimize water use. Implementing features like swales, rain gardens, and water-efficient plantings reflects an advanced understanding of permaculture principles for water resilience.

Technological Integration for Water Resilience: Smart Solutions for Tomorrow

The integration of technology into water prepping strategies represents a significant evolution in preparedness. Advanced prepping involves harnessing smart solutions and cutting-edge technologies to enhance water resilience. From IoT-based water monitoring systems to innovative desalination techniques, staying abreast of technological advancements ensures individuals are equipped to face future challenges.

IoT-based water monitoring systems provide real-time data on water quality, usage patterns, and potential leaks. Integrating these systems into homes or community infrastructures enables proactive water management, reducing waste and ensuring optimal resource utilization. Advanced preppers embrace the connectivity and data insights offered by IoT to make informed decisions about their water supply.

Innovative desalination technologies continue to evolve, offering efficient and sustainable solutions for converting seawater into freshwater. Advanced preppers are attentive to these developments, exploring portable desalination devices and scalable desalination systems that may become integral components of future water prepping strategies. Technological advancements in desalination contribute to the resilience of coastal communities and those facing water scarcity near saltwater sources.

Community Collaboration for Water Security: Strengthening the Collective Front

The future of water prepping extends beyond individual readiness to a collective front where communities collaborate for water security. Advanced prepping involves fostering a sense of shared responsibility, creating community water plans, and engaging in collaborative initiatives. Building resilient communities that can withstand and adapt to changing water dynamics is a cornerstone of future-focused water prepping.

Community water plans, as advanced prepping tools, integrate the expertise of community members, local authorities, and relevant stakeholders. These plans go beyond individual preparedness, encompassing shared infrastructure, emergency response strategies, and sustainable water management practices. Advanced preppers actively participate in the development and implementation of community water plans, recognizing the collective strength in unity.

Collaborative initiatives for water security involve networking with neighboring communities, sharing resources, and participating in regional water resilience projects. Advanced preppers understand the importance of regional cooperation, especially in scenarios where water resources transcend individual boundaries. Building alliances, sharing knowledge, and contributing to larger water security initiatives position communities as proactive agents in shaping a water-resilient future.

In essence, mastering advanced water survival skills involves a multifaceted approach that encompasses physical techniques, psychological resilience, and strategic foresight. From harvesting water from unconventional sources to understanding the mental aspects of survival, individuals equipped with advanced skills navigate water scarcity challenges with confidence.

Expert tips for extreme water emergency situations elevate survival capabilities, offering strategies for unprecedented challenges. Whether through emergency water distillation, atmospheric water harvesting, or advanced filtration methods, individuals with advanced skills can thrive in environments where others might falter.

Evolving water prepping skills for the future requires a paradigm shift towards sustainable practices, technological integration, and community collaboration. By embracing regenerative approaches, staying abreast of technological advancements, and actively participating in community water initiatives, individuals contribute to a resilient water future.

Thriving in the fluid landscape of water survival demands a continuous commitment to learning, adapting, and innovating. As the world grapples with the uncertainties of climate change and environmental shifts, individuals with advanced water survival skills become pioneers in shaping a future where water resilience is not just a skill set but a way of life.

11

Conclusion

In the realm of preparedness, "The New Prepper's Water Survival Bible" stands as an indispensable guide, weaving together the threads of knowledge, foresight, and resilience. As we navigate an era of evolving challenges, this comprehensive manual emerges as a beacon, illuminating the path toward water security in the face of uncertainty. The profound journey through chapters exploring water sourcing, purification, and advanced survival skills mirrors the profound responsibility we bear for our own well-being and that of our communities.

This "Water Survival Bible" is not just a compendium of techniques; it is a call to action—a reminder that water, the essence of life, is both a finite resource and an enduring force. From the basics of water storage to the intricacies of crafting sustainable futures, each chapter embodies the spirit of preparedness as a transformative practice. It transcends the immediate challenges, guiding individuals to evolve their skills, adapt to changing conditions, and become stewards of this vital element.

The profound significance lies not just in the pragmatic wisdom shared within these pages but in the philosophy it imparts—a philosophy of self-reliance, community collaboration, and a resilient mindset. As the world grapples with environmental shifts and global uncertainties, this guide serves as a testament to the enduring power of knowledge and preparedness. It calls upon us to embrace the responsibility of securing our water future, not merely as preppers but as guardians of the life-sustaining essence that flows through every aspect of our existence.

In the profound conclusion of this Water Survival Bible, it becomes evident that preparedness is not a momentary endeavor but a lifelong commitment. The call to evolve our water prepping skills for the future resonates as a timeless directive, urging us to adapt, innovate, and foster a sense of collective responsibility. As we close these pages, the profound echoes of its teachings linger—a reminder that, in the fluid landscape of survival, profound preparedness is not just a necessity; it is a profound act of resilience, wisdom, and enduring stewardship.